Mary Musgrove
Bringing People Together

Torrey Maloof

Consultants

Regina Holland, Ed.S., *Henry County Schools;*
Christina Noblet, Ed.S., *Paulding County;*
School District; **Jennifer Troyer,** *Paulding*
County Schools; **David Proctor,** *Muscogee*
(Creek) Cultural Advisor; **John Ross,** *Certified*
Cherokee Language Teacher; **Karen Coody**
Cooper, M.A., *Cherokee Historian*

Publishing Credits

Rachelle Cracchiolo, M.S.Ed., *Publisher*
Conni Medina, M.A.Ed., *Managing Editor*
Emily R. Smith, M.A.Ed., *Series Developer*
Diana Kenney, M.A.Ed., NBCT, *Content Director*
Torrey Maloof, *Editor*
Courtney Patterson, *Multimedia Designer*

Image Credits: pp. 2, 6, 20, 24, 26, 31 Courtesy of Ed
Jackson; pp. 11, 17 Granger; p. 16 Clipart Courtesy of
FCIT; p. 5 LOC [LC-USZ62-1857]; p. front cover, 7–9,
21 North Wind Pictures; p. 22 National Park Service;
p. 25 Courtesy of Hargrett Rare Book and Manuscript
Library/University of Georgia Libraries; p. 2, 13, 20, 27
Timothy J. Bradley; All other images from iStock and/or
Shutterstock.

Library of Congress Cataloging-in-Publication Data

Names: Maloof, Torrey, author.
Title: Mary Musgrove : bringing people together / Torrey
Maloof.
Description: Huntington Beach, CA : Teacher Created
Materials, 2016. |
   Includes index. | Audience: Grades K to 3.?
Identifiers: LCCN 2015042469 | ISBN 9781493825578
(pbk.)
Subjects: LCSH: Musgrove, Mary, 1700-1765--Juvenile
literature. | Creek
   Indians--Biography--Juvenile literature. |
   Princesses--Georgia--Biography--Juvenile literature. |
   Women--Georgia--Biography--Juvenile literature. |
   Georgia--History--Colonial period, ca.
1600-1775--Juvenile literature.
Classification: LCC E99.C9 M24 2016 | DDC
975.004/973850092--dc23
LC record available at http://lccn.loc.gov/2015042469

Teacher Created Materials

5301 Oceanus Drive
Huntington Beach, CA 92649-1030
http://www.tcmpub.com

ISBN 978-1-4938-2557-8
© 2017 Teacher Created Materials, Inc.
Printed in China
Nordica.022020.CA21902153

Table of Contents

Breaking the Mold

Life for women in the **colonies** (KAHL-uh-neez) was not easy. Women had very few **rights**. They could not own land. They could not vote.

Women worked very hard. They took care of the children. They cleaned their homes. They cooked, farmed, and made clothes. But Mary Musgrove was different. She was a businesswoman.

The Colonies

Long ago, the United States was just 13 colonies. The king of Great Britain ruled them.

Georgia was the last colony to be founded.

More Rights

Creek women had more rights than colonial women. They even owned their own homes.

Young Mary

Mary was born around 1700. Her mother was a Creek Indian. Her father was a white man. He was a **trader** from England.

Mary grew up in two different worlds. When she was young, she lived with her mother. She learned about the **customs** of the Creek.

Two Names

Mary's Creek name was Coosaponakeesa (KOO-sah-puh-nay-KEE-suh). It means "lovely fawn."

HELLO
my name is

Coosaponakeesa

Creek Indians

When Mary was about 10 years old, she went to live with her father. He lived in South Carolina. There, she learned about the life of a colonist. She learned to speak English. And she learned about trade!

Back then, the Creek would trade with colonists. The Creek traded deerskin for guns or cloth. Or they traded for items made of metal, such as kettles and cooking pans.

Deerskin was a common trading item.

Starting a Business

When Mary was older, she met a man named John Musgrove. He was a trader. The two got married.

Together, they started a trading post. It was called Cowpens. It was near the Savannah River. It was a place where people could meet and trade goods.

Savannah River

Did You Hear the News?

Trading posts were also places where people heard about current events. Remember, there was no TV or Internet!

What made Mary and John's trading post so **unique** (yoo-NEEK)? Mary! Her special skills made it a big success.

Mary had **experience** with trade. She had a lot of knowledge about the business. She knew how it worked. She had learned a lot from her father.

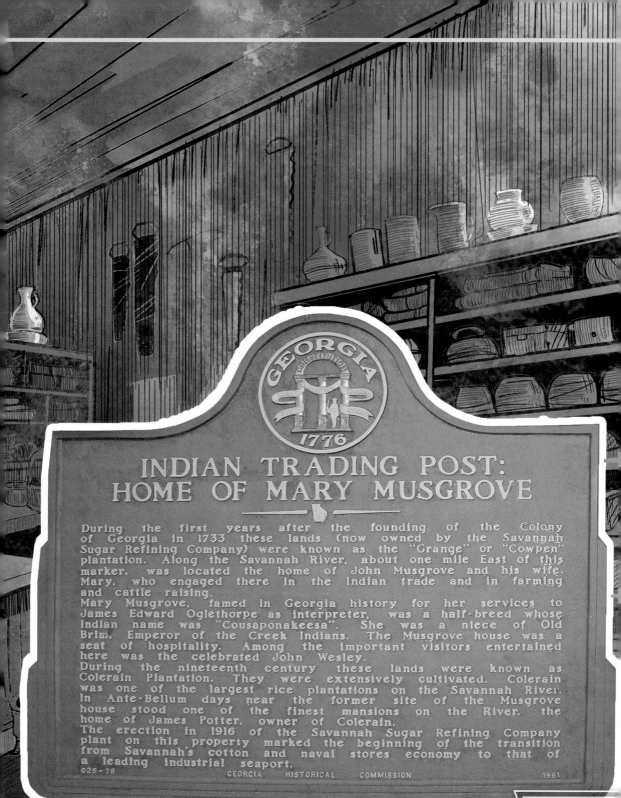

INDIAN TRADING POST:
HOME OF MARY MUSGROVE

During the first years after the founding of the Colony of Georgia in 1733 these lands (now owned by the Savannah Sugar Refining Company) were known as the "Grange" or "Cowpen" plantation. Along the Savannah River, about one mile East of this marker, was located the home of John Musgrove and his wife, Mary, who engaged there in the Indian trade and in farming and cattle raising.

Mary Musgrove, famed in Georgia history for her services to James Edward Oglethorpe as interpreter, was a half-breed whose Indian name was "Cousaponakeesa". She was a niece of Old Brim, Emperor of the Creek Indians. The Musgrove house was a seat of hospitality. Among the important visitors entertained here was the celebrated John Wesley.

During the nineteenth century these lands were known as Colerain Plantation. They were extensively cultivated. Colerain was one of the largest rice plantations on the Savannah River. In Ante-Bellum days near the former site of the Musgrove house stood one of the finest mansions on the River, the home of James Potter, owner of Colerain.

The erection in 1916 of the Savannah Sugar Refining Company plant on this property marked the beginning of the transition from Savannah's cotton and naval stores economy to that of a leading industrial seaport.

025-78   GEORGIA HISTORICAL COMMISSION   1961

Mary's strong bond with the Creek also helped her business. The Creek were her family. They knew Mary well. They trusted her. This made them more willing to trade with her.

Also, Mary could speak two languages. This was a very useful skill. She helped two groups of people talk to each other. She helped them make good trades. She made sure the trades were fair.

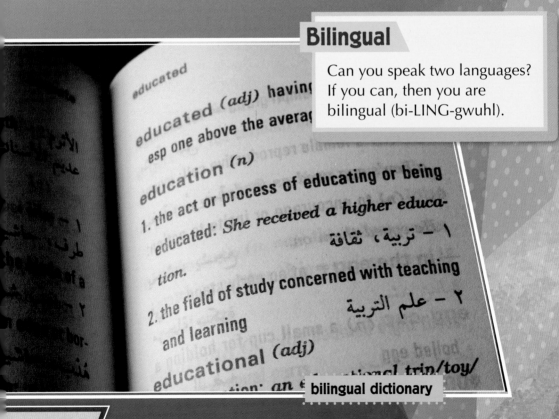

Bilingual

Can you speak two languages? If you can, then you are bilingual (bi-LING-gwuhl).

bilingual dictionary

This is one artist's idea of how Mary might have looked.

A New Friend

In 1733, new **settlers** came to the region. They were from Great Britain. Their leader's name was James Oglethorpe. He wanted to build a new town. He would call it Savannah. But there was a problem.

American Indians were already living there. James did not want to fight with them. He wanted to find a way to share the land. He wished to speak with them. But he did not know how.

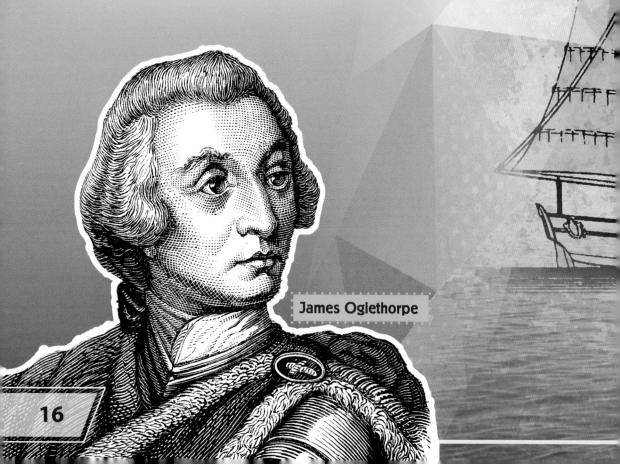

James Oglethorpe

James and the colonists traveled on a ship like this one. It was called the *Anne*.

Mary told James she would help him. She would be his **translator**. She would speak to the Yamacraw (YAH-muh-kraw). That was the name of the local **tribe** of American Indians.

She spoke to their chief, or leader. His name was Tomochichi. They talked about James's plan. She told him James wanted to be friends. She said he would respect their way of life.

Yamacraw

People from the Creek and the Yamasee (YAH-muh-see) tribes joined together. The new tribe was called the Yamacraw.

Thanks to Mary's help, the two men made a deal. They signed a **treaty**. After that, all three of them stayed friends.

Later, Mary's husband died. Mary moved the trading post. She wanted it to be closer to Savannah. She thought she would have more customers there. She was right! Soon, she was very busy. Many more people came to trade goods.

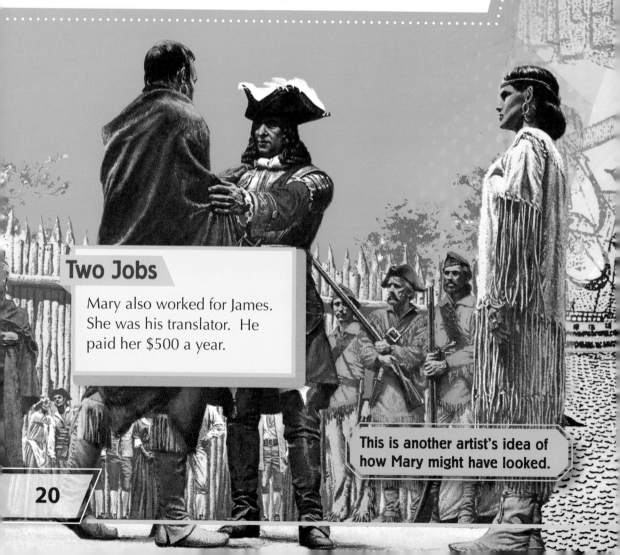

Two Jobs

Mary also worked for James. She was his translator. He paid her $500 a year.

This is another artist's idea of how Mary might have looked.

early Savannah

The Savannah River

More Trading Posts

From 1737 to 1744, Mary got married two more times. But she did not stop working. Her business was doing well.

Soon, Mary set up a second trading post. It was near a fort. A fort is where soldiers live. It was called Mount Venture. Later, she set up a third post! It was called the Forks. The post was given this name because it was built where two rivers met.

Mount Venture may have looked like this fort.

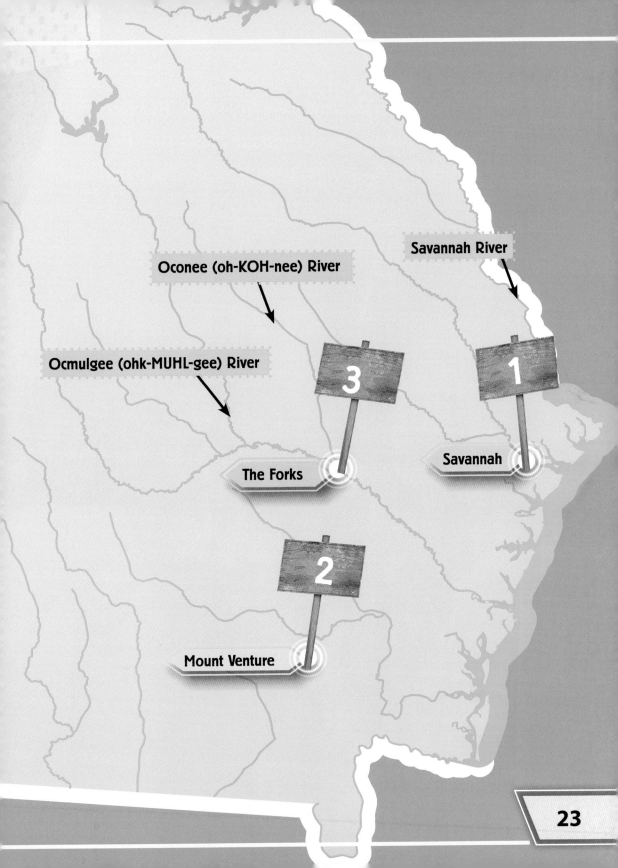

Savannah River

Oconee (oh-KOH-nee) River

Ocmulgee (ohk-MUHL-gee) River

3

1

The Forks

Savannah

2

Mount Venture

Meanwhile, Mary's tribe gave her land. But Great Britain said she did not have rights to it. At that time it was against British law for people to own land. They said that only **nations** could own land.

Mary didn't give up. She kept fighting. It took more than 10 years. In 1759, she was given some of the land, but not all of it. A few years later, she died.

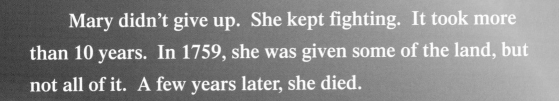

This legal claim argues that Mary and her husband should have the right to own land.

Wealthy Woman

By 1739, Mary was one of the richest women in Georgia.

Bridging the Gap

Mary led an amazing life. She was smart. She worked hard. And she had good business sense.

Mary also had a unique gift. She was able to help people get along. She did this through language. She brought different worlds together. She helped keep the peace.

Georgia would not be what it is today without Mary Musgrove.

Mary translates for Tomochichi and James Oglethorpe.

Mary Lives On

In 2002, archaeologists (ahr-kee-AHL-uh-jists) found Mary's first trading post. About 30,000 artifacts were found at the site!

Send It!

Mary helped groups of people get along. She helped people understand each other. She used language to do it.

Do you know someone like Mary? Write that person a thank-you letter. Tell that person why he or she is so special. Then, send your letter!

Glossary

colonies—areas ruled by a country far away

customs—traditional behaviors or actions of a group of people

experience—skill or knowledge that you get by doing something

nations—large areas of land that are controlled by their own governments

rights—things that a person is allowed to have and do

settlers—people who go to live in a new place where there are few other people

trader—a person who buys, sells, or trades goods

translator—a person who changes words in one language into a different language

treaty—a deal that is made between two or more countries or groups

tribe—a group of people who have the same language, customs, and beliefs

unique—something that is unlike anything else

Index

GEORGIA

1776

INDIAN TRADING POST:
HOME OF MARY MUSGROVE

During the first years after the founding of the Colony
of Georgia in 1733 these lands (now owned by the Savannah
Sugar Refining Company) were known as the "Grange" or "Cowpen"
plantation. Along the Savannah River, about one mile East of this
marker, was located the home of John Musgrove and his wife,
Mary, who engaged there in the Indian trade and in farming
and cattle raising.
Mary Musgrove, famed in Georgia history for her services to
James Edward Oglethorpe as interpreter, was a half-breed whose
Indian name was "Cousaponakeesa". She was a niece of Old
Brim, Emperor of the Creek Indians. The Musgrove house was a
seat of hospitality. Among the important visitors entertained
here was the celebrated John Wesley.
During the nineteenth century these lands were known as
Colerain Plantation. They were extensively cultivated. Colerain
was one of the largest rice plantations on the Savannah River.
In Ante-Bellum days near the former site of the Musgrove
house stood one of the finest mansions on the River, the
home of James Potter, owner of Colerain.
The erection in 1916 of the Savannah Sugar Refining Company
plant on this property marked the beginning of the transition
from Savannah's cotton and naval stores economy to that of
a leading industrial seaport.
025-78   GEORGIA   HISTORICAL   COMMISSION

Your Turn!

What Would You Trade?

Imagine you are living during the time of Mary Musgrove. What would you trade at a trading post? What goods would you need to survive? Write a journal entry about your visit to the trading post.

A graduate of Purdue University, Michelle has been a Sales Executive at AT&T for the past 22 years. She lives in Branchburg, NJ with her husband Frank, their daughter Julia and their son Liam. Julia, now 14, outgrew her dairy allergy at the age of 12. Julia's cousin, Kayla, is still severely allergic to dairy, as is Julia, to nuts. The family has always been very supportive. Julia's Aunt, Heather Hug, an artist from Chicago, provided all the illustrations for Allergic Like Me.

CPSIA information can be obtained
at www.ICGtesting.com
Printed in the USA
LVIC05n2217030314
375943LV00006B/18